Yellowstone & Grand Teton
Activity Book

by Paula Ellis, illustrations by Shane Nitzsche

This book is dedicated to the men and women who worked to set aside and preserve the national parks for all of us to enjoy.

~Paula

Cover design by Jonathan Norberg
Book design by Lora Westberg

10 9 8 7 6 5

Copyright © 2011 by Paula Ellis
Published by Adventure Publications
An imprint of AdventureKEEN
330 Garfield Street South
Cambridge, Minnesota 55008
(800) 678-7006
www.adventurepublications.net
All rights reserved
Printed in U.S.A.

ISBN 978-1-59193-356-4 (pbk.)

Yellowstone National Park

 Look for this picture of the Roosevelt Arch to find pages filled with fun facts and activities about Yellowstone National Park.

- Yellowstone became our country's first national park on March 1, 1872, when President Ulysses Grant signed a bill protecting it "for the benefit and enjoyment of the people."

- Yellowstone National Park sits atop one of the world's largest active volcanoes. The underground volcano is why there are bubbling mudpots, turquoise hot springs, steamy creeks, burping pools and more geysers than anywhere else in the world.

- More than three million people visit Yellowstone every year.

- Six of Yellowstone's mountain peaks are over 11,000 feet high. Eagle Peak is the highest at 11,358 feet.

- Yellowstone is the second-largest national park in the lower 48 states. It covers 2,219,790 acres. That's about as large as Delaware and Rhode Island combined.

- Almost all of Yellowstone is in Wyoming. The rest is in Montana and Idaho.

- Many Native American tribes lived, hunted and traveled through Yellowstone. The Sheepeaters were the only tribe to live in Yellowstone all year long.

- There are more than 300 geysers in Yellowstone. The most powerful geyser is Steamboat Geyser, but it can be quiet for years between eruptions.

- Obsidian is a black, glass-like rock found in Yellowstone. Native Americans traded obsidian and used it to make arrowheads and spear points. You can see obsidian at Obsidian Cliff.

- The national park was named after the Yellowstone River. The river got its name because of the rock walls of a canyon it runs through. The canyon's stone walls appear to be yellow.

- Some money was made in honor of Yellowstone. If you have any quarters, look for Old Faithful and a bison on them. Those are Yellowstone quarters.

- The Continental Divide passes through Yellowstone, separating rivers that run East from rivers that run West. Water in the Snake River runs to the Pacific Ocean, and water in the Yellowstone River runs to the Atlantic Ocean.

Yellowstone Map

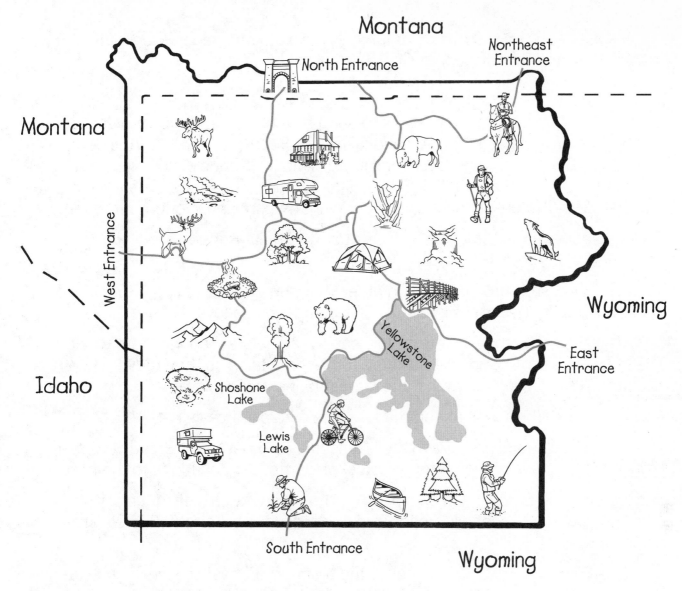

Use the map to find the answers.

What is the name of Yellowstone's largest lake?

☐ Lewis Lake   ☐ Heart Lake   ☐ Yellowstone Lake   ☐ Shoshone Lake

In what state will you find the Roosevelt Arch?

☐ Idaho   ☐ Montana   ☐ Wyoming   ☐ Utah

In what three states is Yellowstone National Park located?

California	Montana	Colorado	Utah	Alaska
Wyoming	Kansas	Arizona	Michigan	New York
Washington	Nebraska	Idaho	Indiana	Florida

(answers on page 62)

Grand Teton National Park

 *Look for the picture of the mountains to find pages filled with fun facts and activities about Grand Teton National Park.*

- Grand Teton National Park has an interesting history. President Calvin Coolidge established part of the land as a national park in February of 1929. President Franklin D. Roosevelt made Jackson Hole a national monument in March of 1943. And finally, on September 14, 1950, President Harry Truman established what we now call Grand Teton National Park by putting the park and monument together.

- The Shoshone Indians referred to the Teton Mountain Range as *teewinot*, meaning "many peaks."

- The peak of Grand Teton is the highest point in the park, reaching 13,770 feet high. Many other peaks are over 12,000 feet above sea level.

- Snow that stays on the mountains for many years is pressed into hard glacial ice. These glaciers carry sand and rock down the mountains as they move. There are 12 named glaciers in the Tetons, the largest being Teton Glacier.

- An average of 191 inches of snow falls in the park each year. That's 16 feet!

- The John D. Rockefeller Jr. Parkway is a scenic road between Grand Teton and Yellowstone. It was named after Mr. Rockefeller for his donations to the park.

- The National Elk Refuge in Jackson Hole protects the area's elk during winter. The refuge is the largest elk preserve in North America. About 9,000 elk stay each winter.

- On June 15, 1971, Bill Briggs became the first person to ski down Grand Teton Peak. Some people call him "the father of extreme skiing in North America."

- The largest lake in Grand Teton National Park is Jackson Lake.

- The park is warm in the summer, with high temperatures averaging about 80 degrees, and cold in the winter, with highs only averaging about 25 degrees.

- The Indian paintbrush is the Wyoming state flower. An American Indian legend says that a warrior tried to paint the sunset. He couldn't do it, so he gave up. He threw his paintbrushes down, and Indian paintbrush flowers grew where the bristles hit the ground.

- Grand Teton National Park offers biking and hiking, excellent rafting down the Snake River, beautiful sunsets over the Tetons and plenty of wildlife, making the park a great place to visit.

Grand Teton Map

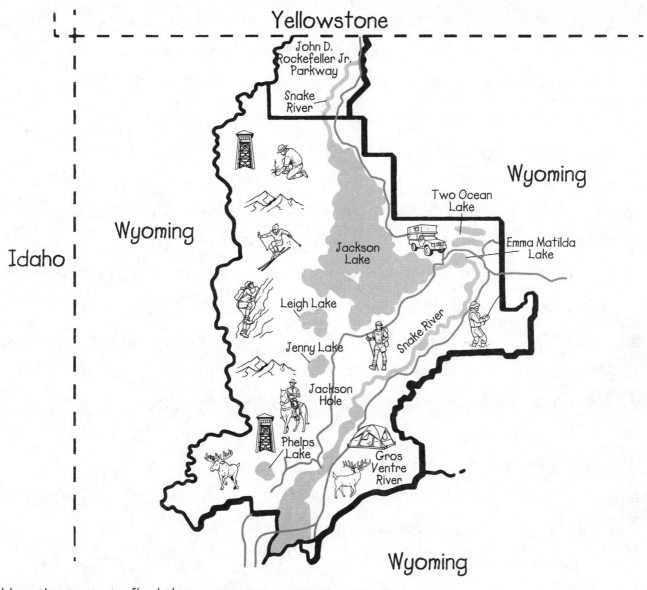

Use the map to find the answers.

In what state is Grand Teton National Park located?

☐ Colorado ☐ Idaho ☐ South Dakota ☐ Wyoming

What large river flows from north to south through the park?

☐ Yellowstone River ☐ Gros Ventre River ☐ Snake River

What do you want to do in Grand Teton National Park?

☐ catch a fish ☐ ride a horse ☐ sleep inside a tent
☐ swim in a lake ☐ see an elk ☐ photograph the mountains
☐ ski down a slope ☐ take a bike ride ☐ become a Junior Ranger

(answers on page 62)

ABCs of Yellowstone & Grand Teton

Take a trip through the alphabet in Yellowstone and Grand Teton.

A is for **Abyss** Pool, the deepest pool in Yellowstone National Park

B is for **Bugle**, the sound elk make in the high country

C is for **Campgrounds**, where people enjoy sleeping in the wilderness

D is for the **Dam** in Jackson Lake, which stores water for farmers

E is for **Elephant** Back Mountain's beautiful view of Yellowstone Lake

F is for Antelope **Flats**, a beautiful meadow in Grand Teton National Park

G is for **Geysers**, which explode throughout Yellowstone

H is for Yellowstone's **Hoodoo** Basin, with rock spires reaching to the sky

I is for **Idaho**, home of the western boundary of Yellowstone

J is for **Jackson** Hole, a beautiful valley at the bottom of the Teton Range

K is for **Kepler** Cascades, waterfalls along Yellowstone's Firehole River

L is for **Lupine**, a silky wildflower that's long and slender

M is for **Montana**, at the northern edge of Yellowstone

N is for **Nature** trails that wind through the parks' wilderness

O is for **Obsidian** Cliffs, made of dark volcanic glass formed from lava

P is for **Pronghorns**, which migrate to the parks for the summer

Q is for Yellowstone's **Quadrant** Mountain of the Gallatin Mountain Range

R is for **Rapids**, which carry rafters down the Snake River in Grand Teton

S is for **Shoshone**, Native Americans who lived in the Yellowstone region

T is for **Trash**, which should always be picked up before you leave

U is for **Ulysses** Grant, who signed the Yellowstone Act on March 1, 1872

V is for **Volcanoes**, underneath the ground of Yellowstone National Park

W is for **Wolves** that live wild and free in the parks

X is for Triangle **X** Dude Ranch—Grand Teton's only guest ranch

Y is for **Yellowstone** River, for which the national park is named

Z is for the **Zigzagging** peaks of the Teton Mountain Range

Grizzly Bear

Grizzly bears roam the parks looking for food and raising their young. You can identify grizzlies by the hump between their shoulders. Their hair is usually brown with white tips, which makes them look "grizzled" or streaked gray. That is how they got their name. Grizzly bears use their large claws to dig dens and to dig up roots to eat.

Do you know what a baby bear is called? _____
BONUS: What is a mother bear called? _____

Camping

Are you ready for a fun adventure? Camping is a great way to enjoy Yellowstone and Grand Teton. Campgrounds are available in both parks, so bring your tent, bike, canoe, backpack and hiking shoes. Get ready to explore, spend time with your family and make new memories.

 You can have plenty of fun setting up a tent in your backyard—or even inside your house!

Lake Names

```
B  W  B  M  O  U  N  T  A  I  N  C
U  H  A  U  J  E  N  N  Y  H  T  A
T  I  S  L  A  N  D  L  E  W  I  S
T  T  I  E  R  V  A  L  L  E  Y  C
E  E  N  C  C  G  W  O  L  F  Z  A
S  B  G  J  H  O  S  N  O  W  V  D
O  T  E  A  L  O  P  E  W  I  C  E
C  G  S  C  A  S  C  X  S  F  T  I
R  R  W  K  H  E  A  R  T  E  R  N
A  E  D  S  H  O  S  H  O  N  E  M
G  B  F  O  R  K  U  D  N  J  Q  U
F  E  R  N  G  L  W  P  E  A  K  D
```

FERN	ICE	TERN
WHITE	GOOSE	YELLOWSTONE
CASCADE	SHOSHONE	JACKSON
GREBE	LEWIS	JENNY
WOLF	HEART	TEAL

**Find the lake names in the puzzle above.
How many bonus words can you find?**

(answers on page 62)

Park Ranger

Park rangers work at the national parks because they care about the animals, the environment and the people who visit. Rangers love to teach people about the land, and they are specially trained to keep visitors and the parks safe. Rangers help to fight fires, perform safety inspections and enforce park rules.

If you have any questions about the parks or if you need assistance, ask a park ranger.

White-water Rafting

The rivers near Yellowstone National Park and Grand Teton National Park are great places for fun and excitement. Paddlers can laugh and scream their way through the bubbling water while surrounded by beautiful scenery. If you brave the rapids with your family and friends, be careful. You're bound to get wet!

 When you're not paddling, watch for bald eagles and golden eagles fishing and eating along the rivers.

Grand Canyon of the Yellowstone

The Grand Canyon of the Yellowstone is one of the most beautiful sights in the park. It is about 20 miles long, up to 4,000 feet wide and as deep as 1,200 feet. The canyon was—and continues to be—shaped by natural forces such as water, wind and earthquakes. This process is called erosion.

In 1869, Charles Cook was one of the first to explore and write about the canyon.

What Does Not Belong in the Parks?

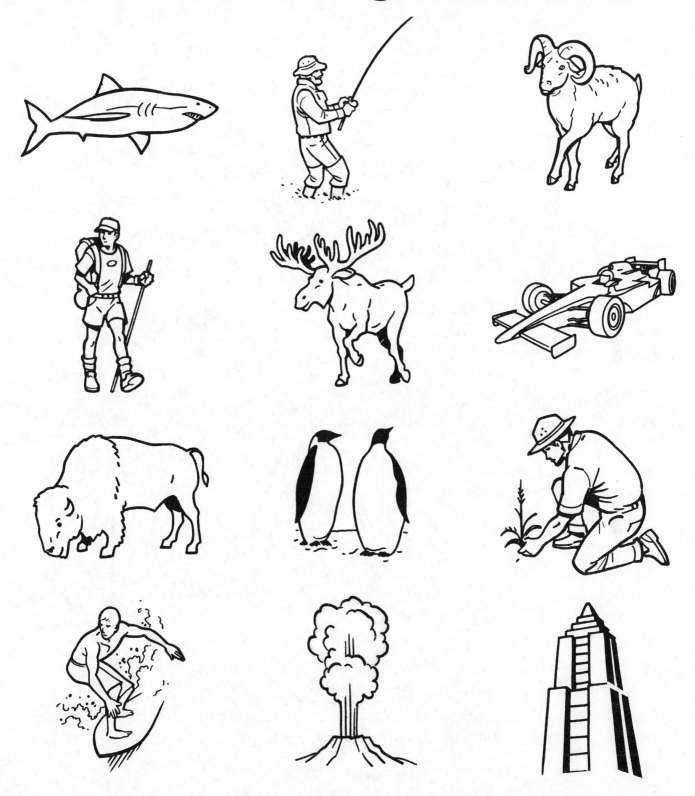

Draw an X over the things you would NOT see in the parks. Circle your favorite things about the parks.

(answers on page 62)

13

Native Americans

Native Americans traveled through the Yellowstone and Grand Teton areas thousands of years before the land became national parks. A Shoshone tribe known as the Sheepeaters was the only tribe to live in the Yellowstone region year-round. Sheepeaters hunted and ate bighorn sheep.

Learn some Shoshone words: *Aishen* **means thank you,** *bungu* **means horse, and** *bozheena* **means bison.**

The First National Park

Early in the 1800s, explorers traveled west and came upon a special land. When they returned, they asked congress to make a law to protect it. Congress passed a bill to make the land into a park. On March 1, 1872, President Ulysses Grant signed the bill into law, and Yellowstone became our first national park.

 National parks have been called "America's best idea" because they preserve the land for everyone to enjoy.

Fun Words

Basin: an enclosed or sheltered low area of land

Butte: a single hill with a flat top and steep sides

Caldera: a large dip in the ground left after a volcano erupts

Crag: a steep, rugged rock sticking out of the mountain

Fork: a spot where a trail divides into two or more directions

Fumarole: a hole where steam shoots out of the ground

Obsidian: a black volcanic rock left from lava that cooled very fast

Plateau: a wide and flat area of high ground

Learning new words can be fun. See how many of these sights you can find in and around the parks.

Fireweed

Fireweed is a beautiful wildflower. It can be white or pink. Fireweed gets its name because it is one of the first plants to grow on burned land after a forest fire. Native Americans ate the young plants and also used them to heal cuts. Nowadays, candy, jelly and even ice cream are sometimes made from fireweed.

True or false? It's okay to pick the flowers you find when you're at a national park.

(answer on page 62)   17

Teddy Roosevelt

Theodore "Teddy" Roosevelt was fascinated by animals and the outdoors. When he became president, he was a friend to the country's wilderness. He established five national parks and 51 wildlife refuges. In 1903, Roosevelt dedicated the arch that marks the north entrance to Yellowstone. It is now called Roosevelt Arch.

 Roosevelt was called the "Great Conservationist." He set aside and protected 194 million acres of land.

Mountain Climbing

Many mountain climbers come to Yellowstone and Grand Teton to climb the parks' hills and mountains. They challenge themselves to climb higher and higher. It is very dangerous, but some people believe the risk is worth it. They say that the best views are at the top, and they feel that getting there is like winning a big game.

Which peak is higher: Yellowstone's Eagle Peak or Grand Teton in Grand Teton National Park?

(answer on page 62)

19

Mudpots

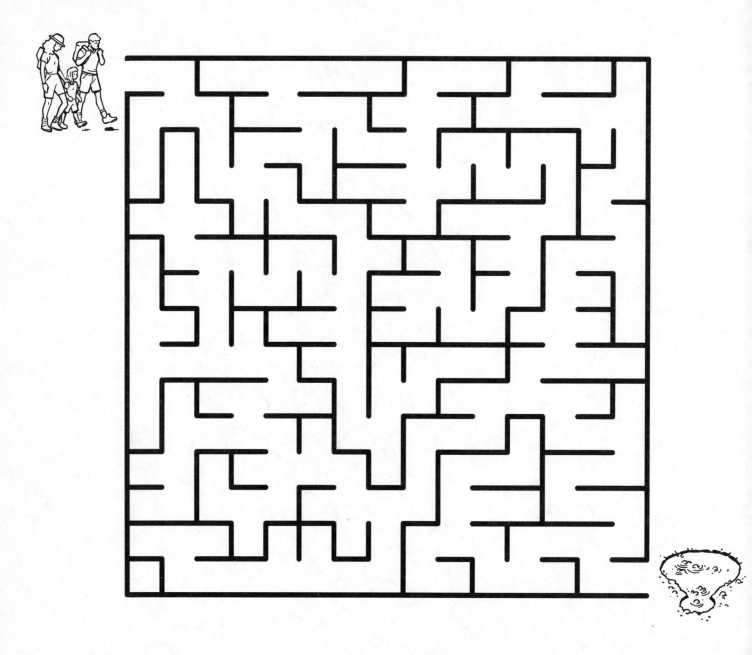

Superhot gases under the ground push up and dissolve rock. The dissolved rock mixes with water and then bubbles into oozing mudpots. "Bloop, bloop, bloop." The ground seems to burp—exploding into showers of mud! It smells like rotten eggs, but that's just the hydrogen sulfide gas coming up from the ground.

Yellowstone's mudpots are very cool to see. Help Hannah and her family find one in the maze above.

(answer on page 62)

Elk

Elk are among the largest types of deer in the world. Only moose are bigger. Male elk, known as bulls, grow antlers and call loudly—or "bugle"—to attract female elk, called cows. Watch for elk grazing in meadows in the morning and evening.

 Bull elk lose their antlers at the end of every winter. It takes only three or four months to grow them again.

Old Faithful

Yellowstone's most famous geyser is called Old Faithful. It got its name because it erupts on a fairly regular—or faithful—schedule. It can be hard to guess when geysers will erupt. But Old Faithful shoots about 8,000 gallons of water up to 184 feet high, and it does so about every 60 to 110 minutes.

There are benches around the geyser, but another great place to watch Old Faithful is from Geyser Hill.

Winter Walk

Yellowstone and Grand Teton are beautiful in the winter. Falling snow lays a blanket of white over the parks. Rangers and scientists study how winter affects the parks, and they examine the many challenges animals face in finding food and staying warm.

Follow the ranger on a snowshoe walk. Dress warmly and watch for tracks in the snow.

(answer on page 62)

Antlers and Horns

Antlers grow on males of the deer family, including moose and elk. Antlers are part of the skull and made of bone, but they fall off each year. Horns are made from bone and a fingernail-like material. Bison and bighorn sheep have horns, which don't fall off but continue to grow as long as the animals live.

Draw a second antler or horn to match the first one on each animal above.

Teton Range

The Teton Range is a group of peaks in the middle of the Rocky Mountains. The range is 40 miles long and 15 miles wide, all within Grand Teton National Park. The tallest peaks are called the Cathedral Group because they look like the pointed tops of a cathedral. The Grand Teton is the highest peak, at 13,770 feet.

Grand Teton is the tallest mountain in the Teton Range. Draw a mountain climber at its peak.

Roosevelt Arch

$$\overline{6}\ \overline{15}\ \overline{18}\ \overline{20}\ \overline{8}\ \overline{5}\ \ \overline{2}\ \overline{5}\ \overline{14}\ \overline{5}\ \overline{6}\ \overline{9}\ \overline{20}\ \ \overline{1}\ \overline{14}\ \overline{4}$$

$$\overline{5}\ \overline{14}\ \overline{10}\ \overline{15}\ \overline{25}\ \overline{13}\ \overline{5}\ \overline{14}\ \overline{20}\ \ \overline{15}\ \overline{6}\ \ \overline{20}\ \overline{8}\ \overline{5}\ \ \overline{16}\ \overline{5}\ \overline{15}\ \overline{16}\ \overline{12}\ \overline{5}$$

Use the code below to write Yellowstone's welcome as seen on the arch:

1	2	3	4	5	6	7	8	9	10	11	12	13	14	15	16	17	18	19	20	21	22	23	24	25	26
A	B	C	D	E	F	G	H	I	J	K	L	M	N	O	P	Q	R	S	T	U	V	W	X	Y	Z

On April 24, 1903, Teddy Roosevelt laid the cornerstone and dedicated the arch at the north entrance to the park.

   (answer on page 62)

Bison

Some people call them buffalo, but the correct name is bison. They are the largest land animals in North America. You might see bison rolling around in dirt. That is called wallowing. It stops flies from biting them and helps them get rid of dead hair. During winter, bison sweep snow aside with their heads in order to eat grass.

Bison nearly went extinct, but a small herd was protected in Yellowstone. Today, bison are no longer endangered.

Hidden Falls

The trail to Hidden Falls in Grand Teton is one of the most popular hikes in the park—and for good reason. Hidden Falls is an 80-foot-high waterfall near Jenny Lake. When you get there, consider going on to Inspiration Point. And don't forget your camera. The view is spectacular!

 Circle the items above that you would pack in the backpack for a hike to Hidden Falls.

(answers on page 62)

Yellowstone Sand Verbena

The Yellowstone sand verbena has white flowers and grows along the ground like a floormat. Strangely, it only grows in Yellowstone—and no place else on earth. Why it grows in this high elevation and how it survives the winters are mysteries. Scientists think it is because of the thermal activity.

 Yellowstone has many other beautiful wildflowers. The Indian paintbrush is Wyoming's official state flower.

Forest Fires

Lightning starts many forest fires every year. Those are called "natural fires," which can be good. Natural fires burn old, dead trees and plants, making room for new plants and trees. Some forest fires are considered "careless fires." These are the ones started by people. They can be very damaging to the parks.

If you ever see a campfire—or any fire—that no one else is watching, make sure you tell an adult.

Fort Yellowstone

In Yellowstone National Park's early years, the U.S. Army protected it and its wildlife from poachers and other greedy people. At first, the soldiers lived in tents, but they later built Fort Yellowstone. When the army's protection was no longer needed, the fort became Yellowstone's headquarters.

Connect the dots, and help build the officers' house at Fort Yellowstone.

Name the Animals

1. _____

2. _____

3. _____

4. _____

5. _____

6. _____

7. _____

8. _____

**Many animals live in the parks. The fastest is the pronghorn.
Write their names on the lines above and circle the pronghorn.**

32 (answers on page 62)

Junior Ranger

If you like exploring the outdoors and learning about plants and animals, you might want to become a Junior Ranger. Pick up a book on how to become one at a visitor center in the parks. When you complete the activities in the book, you will be a National Park Junior Ranger!

 As a Junior Park Ranger, you'll receive an official badge or patch after you review your work with a ranger.

Lower Falls

Lower Falls is the largest and most beautiful waterfall in Yellowstone National Park. The falls is 308 feet high, almost twice as high as Niagara Falls. A green ribbon of water streams down on the side, where the water is deep. The rock walls appear to be a yellow, rust-like color, or "yellow stone."

 Color the yellow rocks along the cliffs and the rainbow at the bottom of Lower Falls.

Winter Words

```
F  R  E  S  K  A  T  E  A  R  S  W
R  J  P  H  W  E  A  T  H  E  R  A
E  Q  G  I  C  E  H  S  M  T  H  L
E  F  A  V  A  L  A  N  C  H  E  S
Z  S  T  E  P  Z  T  O  C  O  A  T
E  K  X  R  Y  C  C  W  X  M  T  E
W  I  N  T  E  R  O  M  Q  I  H  A
S  L  U  S  H  P  L  O  W  T  E  M
D  O  G  S  L  E  D  B  I  T  R  O
A  D  U  N  B  K  G  I  N  E  J  R
Y  F  R  O  S  T  L  L  D  N  T  S
S  N  O  W  S  H  O  E  V  S  G  H
```

STEAM	AVALANCHE	SKI
WEATHER	SNOWMOBILE	SKATE
WINTER	SNOWSHOE	FREEZE
FROST	MITTENS	PLOW
WIND	SHIVER	DOGSLED

**Find the parks' winter words in the puzzle above.
How many bonus words can you find?**

(answers on page 63)

American Pika

The American pika is small like a hamster. It has brown fur and a tail that's so short you can't see it. The pika is also called a rock rabbit. It lives in the mountains and gathers grasses and flowers to eat. You might see small piles of grass that the pika has set out to dry. It takes the grass into its den for winter.

 Pikas are born blind and helpless, but they grow fast. After just three months, they can gather their own food.

Menor's Ferry

In 1892, William "Bill" Menor came to Jackson Hole near the Tetons. He was the first settler to live on the west side of the Snake River. There were no bridges to get across, so Bill built a ferryboat that was pulled along a cable from one side of the river to the other. It was the only way to cross the river.

When you visit Grand Teton, you can ride across the Snake River on a ferryboat just like Menor's Ferry.

Fill in the Blanks

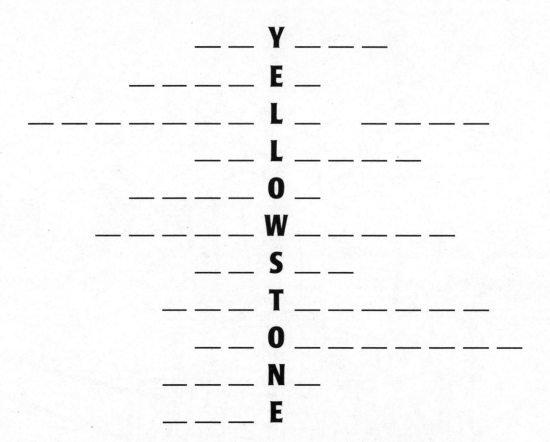

```
_ _ Y _ _ _ _
_ _ _ _ E _
_ _ _ _ _ _ _ L _ _ _ _ _
_ _ _ L _ _ _ _
_ _ _ _ O _ _
_ _ _ _ W _ _ _ _ _ _
_ _ _ S _ _
_ _ _ _ T _ _ _ _ _ _ _
_ _ _ O _ _ _ _ _ _ _ _
_ _ _ _ N _
_ _ _ E
```

1. What shoots steam and water out of the ground in Yellowstone?

2. Who works to keep the park protected, making sure people and animals are safe?

3. What is the most common type of tree in the park?

4. What's below Yellowstone that makes the springs hot and the geysers explode?

5. What is the hot bubbling ground that smells like rotten eggs?

6. What is the largest lake in the park?

7. What animal do people sometimes call a buffalo?

8. What makes the ground shake in Yellowstone, even though you usually can't feel it?

9. What is the only thing you should leave in the park? (Hint: Your feet make them.)

10. Which President signed the bill making Yellowstone a national park?

11. What walking activity do people like to do in Yellowstone?

(answers on page 63)

Chief Joseph

Chief Joseph was a chief of the Nez Perce Indians and a hero to his people. His Indian name was *Hin-mah-too-yah-lat-kekt* or "Thunder Rolling Down the Mountain." He promised to protect his people and their land. He tried to keep peace but failed to prevent his people from being moved to reservations.

Chief Joseph Scenic Highway follows the path taken by the Nez Perce to escape from U. S. soldiers.

Jenny Lake

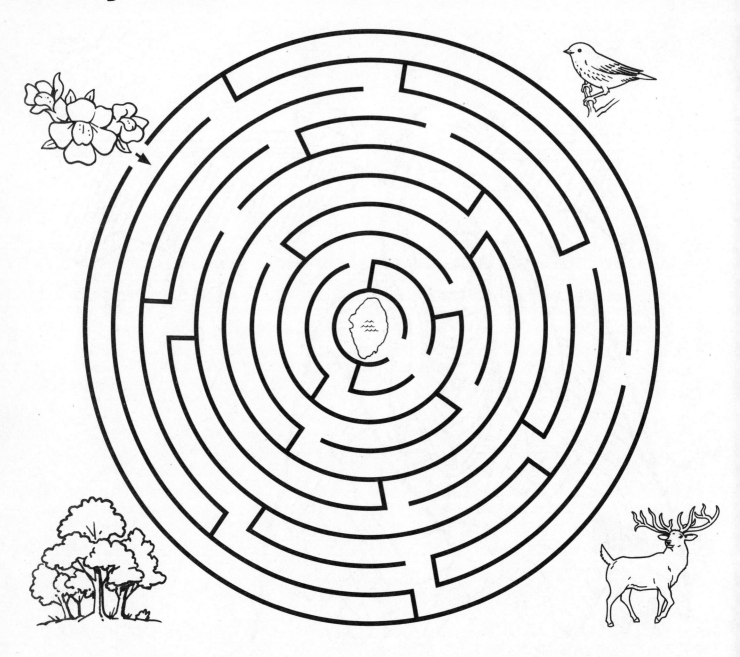

Hiking around Jenny Lake is a favorite activity for Grand Teton visitors. When the warm weather comes, wildflowers such as the yellow monkeyflower bring beautiful colors to the trails. The yellow monkeyflower looks like a monkey's face. Remember: Picking wildflowers in the park is against the rules.

 Help the hiker find the way from the yellow monkey-flower to Jenny Lake.

40 (answer on page 63)

How a Geyser Works

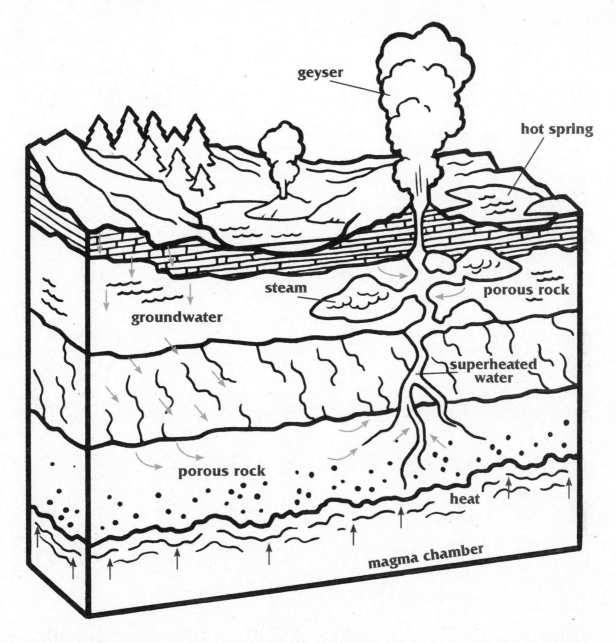

geyser

hot spring

steam

porous rock

groundwater

superheated water

porous rock

heat

magma chamber

There's a volcano far beneath the ground of Yellowstone. It heats underground pockets of water, causing the water's molecules to expand and move faster. This creates a lot of pressure. When the pressure becomes too great, it erupts— shooting hot water and steam into the air, forming a geyser.

 Thanks to all of that underground pressure, you'll find more than 300 geysers in Yellowstone National Park.

Grand Teton Words

```
A S N A K E R I V E R H
X W Y O M I N G B C O I
G C L T O F A L L S C K
L A S F U N E D B I K E
A M V K N B I S O N E L
C P Q G T C L I M B F K
I I T P A A C O L T E R
E N R E I N W E S T L A
R G A A N Y T R A I L N
J A C K S O N H O L E G
A M K R A N J F N H R E
Y D S U M M I T P U Z R
```

SUMMIT   SNAKE RIVER   CLIMB
GLACIER   JACKSON HOLE   TRACKS
WYOMING   ROCKEFELLER   BISON
MOUNTAIN   CANYON   RANGER
PEAK   TRAIL   COLTER

Find words in the puzzle above about Grand Teton National Park. How many bonus words can you find?

42

(answers on page 63)

Horseback Riding

Would you like to explore the parks with a real cowboy? Some people do just that by taking a guided tour on horseback. It's a unique way to experience the parks. Visitors can ride all day or just for an hour. The cowboys help people find wild animals, beautiful wildflowers, valleys, streams and more amazing sights.

Riddle: A cowboy rode into town on Friday. The next day he rode out of town on Friday. How did he do that?

(answer on page 63)

Lodgepole Pine

The lodgepole pine is the most common type of tree in Yellowstone and Grand Teton. Almost all of Yellowstone's land is covered by them, and most of the trees in Grand Teton are lodgepole pines. Forest fires help to spread lodgepole pines. Heat causes the trees' seeds to drop, creating new trees.

Can you guess what Native Americans built using poles made from lodgepole pine trees?

  (answer on page 63)

Protect the Parks

National parks are here for us to enjoy. They are part of our history. You can help save the parks for future generations by being responsible. Care about and respect the parks, the animals and others. By learning the rules and laws of the parks, you can be a friend to some of our country's greatest natural treasures.

Protect our environment for others to enjoy. In the picture above, cross out five things that hurt the parks.

(answers on page 63)

Moose

The moose is the largest member of the deer family. You might see moose eating water plants in streams or eating twigs and leaves beside willow trees. Moose are dark brown, with long legs to walk through thick marshes and deep snow. Watch for the majestic moose throughout the parks.

Moose are dangerous animals. Never approach one, and never ever try to feed one!

Fill in the Blanks

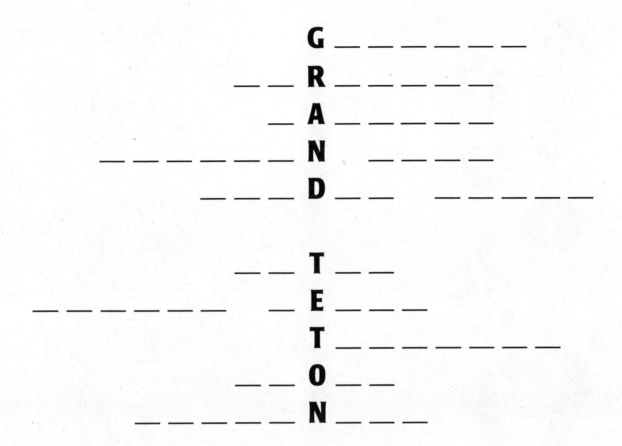

G _ _ _ _ _ _ _

_ _ R _ _ _ _ _

_ A _ _ _ _ _

_ _ _ _ _ N _ _ _ _ _

_ _ _ D _ _ _ _ _ _

_ _ T _ _

_ _ _ _ _ _ E _ _ _

_ T _ _ _ _ _ _

_ _ O _ _ _

_ _ _ _ _ N _ _ _

1. What do you call a large river of slow moving ice?

2. What wildflower is one of the first plants to grow after a forest fire?

3. What do people use a tent for in the park?

4. What valley is at the bottom of the Teton Mountains?

5. What waterfall near Jenny Lake is one of the most popular in the park?

6. What should you drink a lot of on hot days in the park?

7. How did the early settlers cross the Snake River?

8. What did the Native Americans call the Teton Mountain Range?

9. What animal, the largest of the deer family, might you see in the park?

10. What happens when there is too much snow on the mountains?

(answers on page 63)

Who's Been Walking?

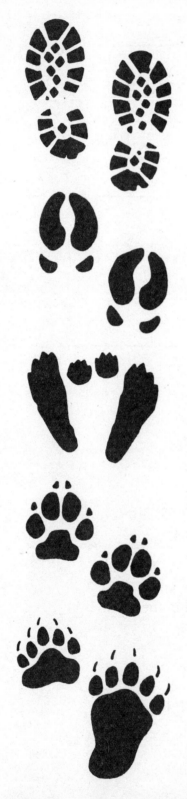

As you hike in the parks, watch for tracks to see who else has been there. Can you match the tracks above with the animal?

(answers on page 63)

Geologist

Geologists are scientists who study the solids and liquids that make up our earth. In Yellowstone, geologists study the land to learn about its history and to understand geysers, hot springs and mudpots. In Grand Teton, they study old rocks and one of the newest mountain ranges in North America.

There are up to 3,000 earthquakes in Yellowstone every year, but most of them can't even be felt!

Winter Weather

The parks are high in the mountains and that means lots of deep snow and cold weather. Many people come to the parks to snowshoe, cross-country ski and snowmobile, but getting to the parks can be a problem. Giant snow-blowers work hard to clear the roads, so people can enjoy winter in the parks.

 On February 9, 1933, the temperature in Yellowstone reached 66 degrees below zero—the parks' coldest day.

Petrified Tree

There are many strangely beautiful things in Yellowstone, and one of the strangest is a petrified tree. It looks like a tree made out of rock! Many years ago it was a tree, but ash from a volcano buried it. The tree's buried wood decayed, and minerals replaced the wood—turning it into stone.

Connect the dots above to see the petrified tree near Tower Junction.

Trumpeter Swan

The trumpeter swan is the largest waterfowl in North America. It gets its name from its call, which sounds like a trumpet. Trumpeter swans dip their heads underwater to eat plants and small fish, a process called dabbling. These birds used to be hunted for their feathers, but now the parks work to help save trumpeter swans.

Male swans have wingspans up to seven feet. That means their wings stretch wider than the height of a tall adult!

Fishing

Yellowstone and Grand Teton's many lakes and rivers are filled with fish. The parks' most common type of fish are called cutthroat trout. Thousands of fishermen come to fish for trout, which can be up to 26 inches long. Cutthroat trout are named for the colored streaks on the sides of their jaws.

True or false? Yellowstone's Fishing Bridge is a great place to catch fish.

(answer on page 64)

Explore Yellowstone

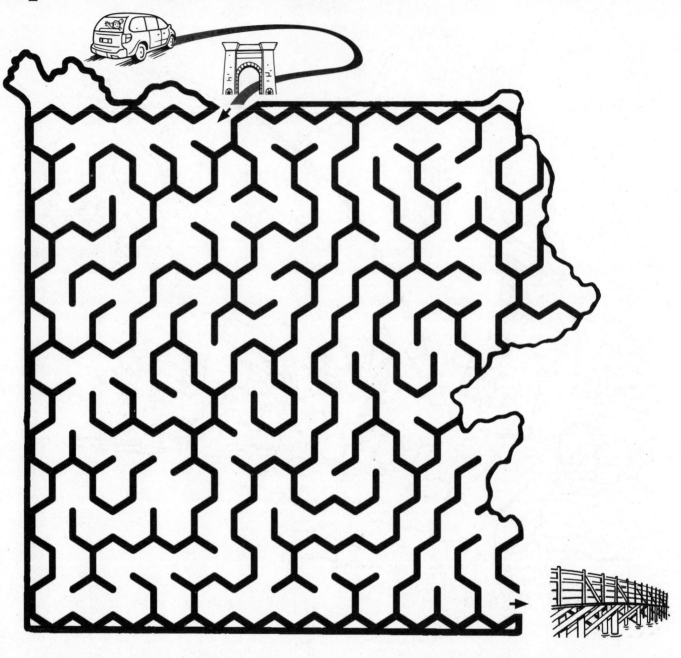

Sarah's family has planned a trip to explore Yellowstone. They will enter through the Roosevelt Arch and make their way to the Fishing Bridge. Sarah's family also plans to check out the visitor center, the mudpots, Old Faithful, the Grand Canyon and the Yellowstone River. That sounds like fun!

 Help Sarah and her family find their way from the Roosevelt Arch to the Fishing Bridge.

Stagecoach Ride

Over 100 years ago, the best way to travel in the Yellowstone and Grand Teton area was by stagecoach. Visitors enjoyed seeing the country's national parks by stagecoach until 1917, when stagecoaches were no longer used. Today you can ride a stagecoach in the parks, just like early visitors did.

A stagecoach was a carriage, pulled by horses, that carried passengers and supplies over rugged trails.

Bingo

If you see one of the people, places, animals or objects on the bingo card, mark it with an X. Be sure to mark the free space in the middle. If you get five Xs in a row, you win! Remember to yell "Bingo!"

B	I	N	G	O
MOUNTAINS	ARCH	GEYSER	BISON	PETRIFIED TREE
PINE TREE	RIVER	RV	MUDPOT	BRIDGE
MOOSE	RANGER	FREE	YELLOWSTONE QUARTER	HORSEBACK RIDER
ELK	FIREWEED	WATERFALL	STAGECOACH	BEAR
GLACIER	PRONGHORN	LUPINE	BIGHORN SHEEP	CYCLIST

License plate game: Where do the tourists come from? How many different state license plates you can find?

Jackson Hole

In the 1820s, explorers such as David Jackson trapped for furs near Grand Teton. They climbed down steep hills and mountains to get into the valley. This place was named Jackson Hole, although it is not really a "hole." Elk graze there in the winter. Tourists visit to ski, hike and enjoy the scenic beauty.

 The Snake River, in Jackson Hole, got its name from a hand signal made by Shoshone Indians.

Bighorn Sheep

The male bighorn sheep, also called a ram, has horns that weigh up to 30 pounds! Rams use their horns to butt heads or fight. The females, called ewes, have horns too, but their horns are shorter and lighter with smaller curves. Native Americans used bighorn sheep horns to make bows for hunting.

Bighorn sheep have split hooves, so they are better able to climb on the mountains like goats.

Quiz Your Parents

1. Yellowstone National Park is in what three states?

2. What is the highest peak in Yellowstone?

3. What species of tree covers most of the park?

4. What is the fastest mammal in the park?

5. What is the largest mammal in the park?

6. What is the largest lake in Yellowstone?

7. Name the black, glass-like rock found in Yellowstone.

8. For what is Yellowstone named?

9. Which president signed the bill making Yellowstone our first national park?

10. Who helped explore the Grand Canyon of the Yellowstone in 1869?

11. How many geysers can be found in Yellowstone?

12. What famous space movie was filmed partly in Yellowstone?

13. Who is believed to have been the first white man to see Yellowstone?

14. For which president is a famous Yellowstone arch named?

15. In what state is Grand Teton National Park located?

16. What is the longest river in Grand Teton National Park?

17. Who was the first person to ski down Grand Teton Peak?

18. What is the largest lake in Grand Teton National Park?

19. What is the tallest mountain in Grand Teton National Park?

20. What does *teewinot* mean?

(answers on page 64)

John Colter

John Colter was a hunter, trapper and guide. He explored the West with the Lewis & Clark Expedition. He was one of the first white men to see what we now call Yellowstone and Grand Teton. When he returned East and told people about steaming geysers and bubbling mudpots, people thought he was crazy or telling a tall tale.

Colter Bay in Grand Teton and Colter Peak in Yellowstone are named after the mountain man.

Safety & Conservation Quiz

Test your knowledge of safety and conservation tips in the national parks.
Circle ALL of the correct answers for each question below.

1. Why should you obey the park rules?

    A.) The rules are made to keep you safe.

    B.) It is the law.

    C.) You can be an example for other kids.

2. What is the best way to watch wildlife?

    A.) Get as close as you can to them.

    B.) Stay back and watch with binoculars.

    C.) Leave out food so they will come closer.

3. Why should you never feed the animals?

    A.) They don't like our food.

    B.) They could become dangerous and aggressive.

    C.) They will come closer to people and not be afraid anymore.

4. Why should you never get close to wild animals?

    A.) They are dangerous.

    B.) They might try to tickle you.

    C.) They might have babies to protect and could become angry.

5. How can you keep bears from coming to your campsite?

    A.) Keep your food in a bear-proof container.

    B.) Clean up your garbage and put it in trash cans.

    C.) Talk loud or make lots of noise.

    D.) Leave your food out on the picnic table.

6. What is the best way to stay cool on hot days in the parks?

    A.) Wear light-colored clothes.

    B.) Eat lots of candy.

    C.) Drink lots of water.

    D.) Stay in the shade when you can.

(answer on page 64)

Answers

Page 3–Yellowstone Map

Yellowstone

Montana

Wyoming, Montana, Idaho

Page 5–Grand Teton Map

Wyoming

Snake River

Page 7–Grizzly Bear

Cub

Bonus: Sow

Page 9–Lake Names

```
H  W  B  M  O  U  N  T  A  I  N  C
U  H  A  U  J  E  N  N  Y  H  T  A
T  I  S  L  A  N  D  L  E  W  I  S
T  T  I  E  R  V  A  L  L  E  Y  C
E  E  N  C  C  G  W  O  L  F  Z  A
S  B  G  J  H  O  S  N  O  W  V  D
O  C  E  A  N  O  P  E  W  I  C  E
C  G  S  C  A  S  C  X  S  F  T  I
R  R  W  K  H  E  A  R  T  E  R  N
A  E  D  S  H  O  S  H  O  N  E  M
G  B  F  O  R  K  U  D  N  J  Q  U
F  E  R  N  G  L  W  P  E  A  K  D
```

Page 13–What Does Not Belong in the Parks?

Shark, race car, penguin, surfer, skyscraper building

Page 17–Fireweed

False. If everyone did it, there would be none left to enjoy!

Page 19–Mountain Climbing

Grand Teton Peak. It's 13,770 feet high. Eagle Peak is 11,358 feet high.

Page 20–Mudpots

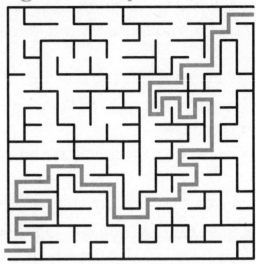

Page 23–Winter Walk

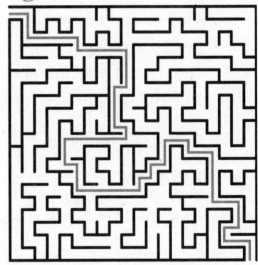

Page 26–Roosevelt Arch

"For the benefit and enjoyment of the people"

Page 28–Hidden Falls

Water bottle, compass, map, whistle, binoculars, camera, first-aid kit

Page 32–Name the Animals

1. Bear, 2. Wolf, 3. Moose,
4. Raccoon, 5. Beaver, 6. Bison,
7. Pika, 8. Pronghorn

Answers

Page 35—Winter Words

```
F R E S K A T E A R S W
R J P H W E A T H E R A
E Q G I C E H S M T H L
E F A V A L A N C H E S
Z S T E P Z T O C O A T
E K X R Y C C W X M T E
W I N T E R O M Q I H A
S L U S H P L O W T E M
D O G S L E D B I N E O
A D U N B K G I N T J R
Y F R O S T L L D S T S
S N O W S H O E V S G H
```

Page 38—Fill in the Blanks

Geyser	Ranger
Lodgepole Pine	Volcano
Mudpot	Yellowstone
Bison	Earthquake
Footprints	Grant
Hike	

Page 40—Jenny Lake

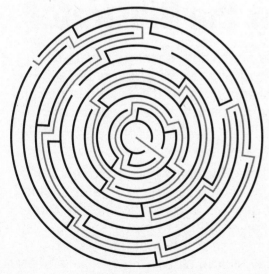

Page 43—Riddle

The name of his horse was Friday!

Page 44—Lodgepole Pine

Native Americans used poles made from lodgepole pines to build teepees to live in.

Page 42—Grand Teton Words

```
A S N A K E R I V E R R H
X W Y O M I N G B C O I K
G C L T O F A L L S C K C
L A S F U N E D B I K E K
A M V K N B I S O N E L
C P Q G T C L I M B F K
I E T P A A C O L T E R
E N R E A N W E S T L A
R G A A I Y T R A I L N
J A C K S O N H O L E G
A M K R A N J F N H R E
Y D S U M M I T P U Z R
```

Page 45—Protect the Parks

trash on the ground

plastic jug in river

fireworks

initials carved in tree

nails in tree

campfire too close to trees

Page 47—Fill in the Blanks

Glacier	Fireweed
Camping	Jackson Hole
Hidden Falls	Water
Menor's Ferry	Teewinot
Moose	Avalanche

Page 48—Who's Been Walking?

Answers

Page 53—Fishing

False. Fishing is not allowed on Fishing Bridge because it is a place where cutthroat trout come to lay their eggs.

Page 54—Explore Yellowstone

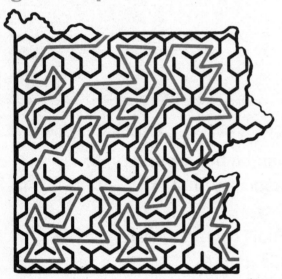

Page 59—Quiz Your Parents

1. Idaho, Montana, Wyoming;
2. Eagle Peak; 3. Lodgepole Pine;
4. Pronghorn; 5. Bison; 6. Yellowstone Lake; 7. Obsidian; 8. Yellow rocks along the Yellowstone River;
9. Ulysses Grant; 10. Charles Cook;
11. More than 300; 12. Star Trek: The Motion Picture; 13. John Colter;
14. Teddy Roosevelt; 15. Wyoming;
16. Snake River; 17. Bill Briggs;
18. Jackson Lake; 19. Grand Teton;
20. Many peaks

Page 61—Safety & Conservation

1. A, B, C	2. B
3. B, C	4. A, C
5. A, B, C	6. A, C, D

About the Author

Paula Ellis grew up in a small town in central Michigan. Her love of the outdoors and travel began at a young age. She is the mother of two children, daughter Heather and son Todd David. Through travel and everyday experiences, she taught them to appreciate, respect and enjoy all of creation.

Paula enjoys being a grandma, exploring the wilderness, traveling and watching her four grandchildren grow and learn about the world in which they live.

She believes children are eager to learn about their environment, whether they're playing in the backyard, traveling across the country or catching bugs on a camping trip. To that end, she strives to encourage children of all ages to see and explore all of the fascinating things around them.

About the Illustrator

Picking up a pencil and drawing on a sheet of paper is one of Shane's first memories, and he has never stopped since! It was no surprise when at a very young age he decided that artwork would be more than his hobby; it would be his lifelong career.

Shane has been fortunate enough to work on many exciting projects in many different fields: from t-shirt designs to comic books and from science fiction paintings to movie storyboards. He has always had a soft spot for making artwork that children can enjoy.

Shane found his home in Portland, OR. He has a wonderful daughter Hannah who has the potential to be a great artist if she works hard. The same can be said for you, no matter what it is you want to do.